HOW DO
POLAR BEARS
STAY WARM?

MARK RIPLEY

press.

New York

Published in 2018 by The Rosen Publishing Group, Inc.
29 East 21st Street, New York, NY 10010

First Edition

Editor: Theresa Morlock
Book Design: Tanya Dellaccio

Photo Credits: Cover, back cover, pp. 1, 3–4, 6–10, 12–18, 20–24 Rebecca R Jackrel/Getty Images; p. 4 Peter Hermes Furian/Shutterstock.com; p. 5 FloridaStock/Shutterstock.com; p. 7 (top) vladsilver/Shutterstock.com; p. 7 (bottom) Helen Birkin/Shutterstock.com; p. 9 (top) Sue Flood/The Images Bank/ Getty Images; pp. 9 (bottom), 12 Alexey Seafarer/Shutterstock.com; p. 11 GUDKOV ANDREY/Shutterstock.com; p. 13 (top) andamanec/ Shutterstock.com; p. 13 (bottom) Belovodchenko Anton/Shutterstock.com; p. 14 Nirut Sampan/Shutterstock.com; p. 15 (top) Aysa_t/Shutterstock.com; p. 15 (bottom) AndreAnita/Shutterstock.com; pp. 16, 17 (bottom) outdoorsman/ Shutterstock.com; p. 17 (top) Elpisterra/Shutterstock.com; p. 19 Michael Nolan/ robertharding/Getty Images; p. 21 (top) Ondrej Prosicky/Shutterstock.com; p. 21 (bottom) Yuma Ishizu/Shutterstock.com; p. 22 FloridaStock/Getty Images.

Cataloging-in-Publication Data
Names: Ripley, Mark.
Title: How do polar bears stay warm? / Mark Ripley.
Description: New York : PowerKids Press, 2018. | Series: How life science works | Includes index.
Identifiers: ISBN 9781508156475 (pbk.) | ISBN 9781508156413 (library bound) | ISBN 9781508156291 (6 pack)
Subjects: LCSH: Polar bear–Juvenile literature.
Classification: LCC QL737.C27 R57 2018 | DDC 599.786-dc23

Manufactured in the United States of America

CPSIA Compliance Information: Batch #BS17PK For Further Information contact Rosen Publishing, New York, New York at 1-800-237-9932

CONTENTS

BEARS OF THE NORTH POLE

At the top of the planet, as far north as north goes, there's an icy-cold ocean with the North Pole near its center. Parts of eight countries surround this ocean, which is covered in floating sea ice 6 to 9 feet (1.8 to 2.7 m) thick. With **temperatures** that dip below -94° Fahrenheit (-70° Celsius), this freezing landscape, called the Arctic, is one of the coldest places on Earth.

What animal could possibly stay warm in this chilly **environment**? The polar bear can! Polar bears are built to survive in the harsh conditions of the North Pole.

ARCTIC CIRCLE

The word "arctic" comes from the Greek word *arktos*, which means "bear." The Arctic got its name from Ursa Minor and Ursa Major, which are bear-shaped constellations, or groups of stars, in the northern sky.

KINGS OF THE FOOD CHAIN

Although the wintry Arctic is a hard place to live, many species, or kinds, of animals are able to survive there. The Arctic **ecosystem** is home to marine creatures such as narwhals and seals and land animals such as caribou and Arctic foxes.

Polar bears are the apex, or top, predator in their ecosystem. They are one of the largest meat-eating land animals in the world and feed mostly on seals. Seals have plenty of fat, which polar bears eat to gain energy. They also eat birds and the remains of dead whales and walruses. Polar bears use sea ice to travel and hunt for food.

Polar bears are very good swimmers. They have **WEBBED** front paws that help them paddle through the water.

HUNTING ON ICE

Polar bears hunt in areas where ice is cracked. It's at these spots that seals swim to the surface to breathe. Polar bears can sniff out seals at a breathing hole up to a mile (1.6 km) away. They may spend hours or even days waiting at a breathing hole before a seal surfaces. They use their sharp teeth and claws to pull seals on shore to eat them.

Polar bears may travel hundreds of miles to find food. Some areas of sea ice are better hunting spots than others. During the summer, when some ice melts and the remaining ice moves, polar bears follow the ice's movement.

After they eat, polar bears leave behind parts of their prey. These remains feed animals that are lower on the food chain, such as Arctic foxes and gulls.

BEAR BEHAVIORS

Each polar bear has its own home **range**. They mark their ranges with scents from their paws. Within these ranges, they spend their time alone, coming together only to **mate**.

Adult bears mate in the spring. In the fall, females dig dens deep in the snow. During winter, they give birth to their cubs in the den. Female polar bears usually have twin cubs that are only about 12 inches (30.5 cm) long and weigh about 1 pound (0.5 kg). Cubs don't leave the den until the spring and spend the first two years of their lives learning from their mothers. Male polar bears don't help raise their cubs.

Polar bears use scents to communicate with and find other bears.

MOTHERS AND CUBS

During the months in the den, mother polar bears don't eat. They may go up to four months without food. They live off fat stored in their body. Mothers need to gain about 440 pounds (200 kg) to have a healthy pregnancy. During this time, they feed their cubs milk from their own body.

When the mother and cubs come out of the den, she searches for sea ice from which to hunt seals. Mothers train their cubs to stalk their prey quietly. They teach cubs how to fight and how to swim. Mother polar bears **protect** their cubs at all costs.

POLAR BEARS REACH ADULTHOOD WHEN THEY'RE ABOUT FIVE YEARS OLD.

ARCTIC ADAPTATIONS

In addition to the skills they learn from their mothers, polar bears have special adaptations, or changes that help them live better in their environment.

A polar bear's fur acts as camouflage, helping it blend in with its snowy surroundings. Its large feet and strong legs help it walk on deep snow and ice and swim for hours. Polar bears' paws have pads on the bottom that keep them from slipping on ice. Polar bears are very fast and can run at speeds of up to 25 miles (40.2 km) per hour. When they catch their prey, their sharp teeth and claws help them tear it apart easily.

Although it looks white, polar bear fur is actually transparent, or clear. Light reflects, or bounces, off the fur, which makes it appear white.

STAYING WARM

Polar bears have three main adaptations to help them stay warm: a layer of fat, black skin, and thick fur. A polar bear's fat layer can be up to 4.3 inches (11 cm) thick. This fat keeps them warm when they're swimming or diving for prey.

The color black absorbs, or takes in and holds, sunlight and turns it into heat. In this way, a polar bear's black skin helps it keep warm. On top of this skin is a thick undercoat of soft fur. A **coarse** layer of fur grows on top of this. This fur helps lock in the bear's body heat.

POLAR BEARS HAVE FUR BETWEEN THEIR TOES. THIS HELPS KEEP THEM WARM AND ALSO KEEPS THEM FROM SLIPPING ON ICE.

COOLING OFF

Polar bears are warm-blooded mammals. Like humans, their average body temperature is 98.6° Fahrenheit (37° Celsius). The special adaptations of polar bears are so good at keeping them warm that sometimes polar bears even overheat!

To keep from overheating, polar bears try to save their energy as much as possible. They can save energy by walking slowly and only running when it's necessary. Part of the reason that polar bears stalk seals at breathing holes is to avoid chasing them. Polar bears can cool off by going for a swim or by lying on their backs and panting.

Polar bears can weigh between 900 and 1,600 pounds (408.2 and 725.8 kg) and be as long as 8 feet (2.4 m).

DANGERS TO POLAR BEARS

Polar bears are one of the many species that have been affected by **global warming**. As global temperatures rise, sea ice is beginning to melt very quickly. Polar bears depend on sea ice to survive and, as a result, their populations have begun to drop. Melting sea ice forces polar bears to swim farther to find places where they can hunt for food, and many are beginning to **starve**.

Other dangers to polar bears include illegal hunting and **habitat** loss due to human activities. Trade ships in the Arctic Ocean can pollute bear habitats. Unless action is taken to save polar bear habitats, they're at risk of becoming **endangered**.

Right now, polar bears are listed as a vulnerable species. That means they are at a high risk of becoming endangered in the wild.

A KEYSTONE SPECIES

At the current rate of climate change, it's possible that two-thirds of the world's polar bears will be gone by the year 2050. Polar bears are a very important part of the Arctic ecosystem. As their population suffers, other animals in the food chain are also affected.

Polar bears are a keystone species, which means that many other species in their ecosystem depend on them for survival. If polar bears disappear from the Arctic, the loss may ruin the entire ecosystem. Polar bears are worth saving for so many reasons! Taking steps to control global warming could change the future of this wonderful animal.

GLOSSARY

coarse: Rough or wiry.

ecosystem: A natural community of living and nonliving things.

endangered: In danger of dying out.

environment: The natural world around us.

global warming: A gradual increase in how hot Earth is. It's believed to be caused by gases that are released when people burn fuels such as gasoline.

habitat: The natural home for plants, animals, and other living things.

mate: To come together to make babies, or one of two animals that come together to make babies.

protect: To keep safe.

range: An open area of land over which animals move and feed.

starve: To suffer or die from hunger.

temperature: How hot or cold something is.

webbed: Having skin between the toes, as ducks, frogs, and other animals that swim do.

INDEX

WEBSITES

Due to the changing nature of Internet links, PowerKids Press has developed an online list of websites related to the subject of this book. This site is updated regularly. Please use this link to access the list: www.powerkidslinks.com/ls/pol